ANOTHER BLACK GIRL MIRACLE

POEMS BY: TONYA INGRAM

not a cult.

los angeles, ca
notacult.media

Printed in the USA

Ingram, Tonya

1st edition.

ISBN: 978-1-945649-07-3

Edited by Jeremy Radin and Safia Elhillo
Cover design by Cassidy Trier
Editorial design by Ian DeLucca

not a cult.
Los Angeles, CA

Printed in the United States of America

this book is for you.

about two weeks ago, my blood levels were so incredibly low that had i not admitted myself to the emergency room, i would have had a heart attack within a few days. what shocked doctors the most was my resilience to stay alive despite every-thing within me barely wanting to hold on. and that's just it. the resilience. the back against the wall instinct. the still breathing mentality. the gotta keep moving prayer. all of it an ode to our healing. it's okay to drag yourself to the end of this week with just enough in you to say 'i made it.' my friend, you made it. to the back end of some expectation long built for you. you are here. yeah, you probably got here with some ailment stuck to your name. or a trail of dust coating your fist, but you came out swinging like a holy roller. like a stun-ning giant. you did that. with your hands still in tremble. with your eyes still in weep. you are everything keeping you alive. i am a woman with a compli-cated story, a complicated disease. for each day there is breath/ love/now, there is the novel of my life turning its page. and that is enough to live for. amen.

Contents

Foreword   1

Cincinnati, Ohio   4

I Am Twenty-Two   5

While Sitting In Central Park I Consider My   9
   Mother's Good Knife

Una Mujer y Su Casa / A Woman and Her House   10

On A Too-Hot Wednesday   11

A Scripture For Delilah   12

Thirteen, or, How OKCupid Told My Mother   13
   I Had the Devil Living Inside of Me

Black Paralysis   16

The Most Poppin' Crotchet Braids   17

The Blonde, The Boulder & The Blues   21

Drowning (The Good Kind)   22

The Black Girl Miracle & The 72 Hour Hold   23

The Saddest Thing   24

The Black Girl Miracle Swipes Right on Tinder   25

The Weekend   26

Proverbs Four: Train   27

I Know the Cold Touch of the Living   28

When The Lights Go Down   29

The Black Girl Miracle Deletes Her Tinder Profile   30

Here Is What Loneliness Tells You   32

Here Is What Love Tells You 33

One Time For The Kid In The Back Of The Class- 34
room Who Stayed Up Playing NBA2K17 Instead
Of Doing Homework

RuPaul Gives The Black Girl Miarcle Her First 37
Lesson In Realness

Beyoncè Gives The Black Girl Miracle Her First 38
Lesson In Healing

Hot Sauce In Our Bag 39

I Am Twenty-Five 41

For Him | Prologue or How My Grandparents 42
Explain 46 Years Of Marriage

For Him | Act I 43

Joy In The Year of Kidney Failure 47

An Open Letter To My Depression 49

Until The Stars Collapse 52

The Black Girl Miracle & The 72 Hour Hold 53
(Continued)

For Him | Act II 54

For Her | Finale 57

The Black Girl Miracle Saw Moonlight & 58
Cannot Stop Crying

On Being Called A Slave During My Acting 59
Class

Dear Discouraged 60

The Black Girl Miracle Tells Her Sister A 61
Secret On The Corner Of 183rd Street
& Walton Avenue

Acknowledgements 65

Foreword

to be black and depressed is often thought to be a con-
tradiction. how can i not be depressed when the names
continue to pile. when the #justicefor_____ continues to
trend. when we chant "black lives matter" and someone
begins to growl.

growing up, i felt the burden of my loneliness. i wept into
my tired pillow and kept the sadness close. i did not want
to alarm. to be sick. the stigma of mental illness plagues
our community. it keeps our heaviness in the dark and
disregards expression in its truest form, when it is diffi-
cult and muddy. i am currently listening to nina simone's
"i wish i knew how it would feel to be free," and i am
reminded of stigma. how if we came to understand what
depression is, how it rattles and scolds and leeches, we
can begin to understand ourselves and how dynamic we
can become as a support system. we begin to understand
what it means to free.

for those who feel the distance, the quiet, know you are
not alone. i am your keeper. i am the hymn in the moment
of chaos. there is much to be celebrated in our skin. there
is much to love about the resilience of our kin. and yet,
there is room to be at the floodgates. to feel everything
and not define ourselves as the outcast. oh, friend, find
me when the ridicule glistens. find me when they tell you
to get over it.

find me when they name depression a false space. find me.

you are not crazy. you are the glow. you are the story of our ancestors and the glory of our future. you are a brilliant storm. you are a body made of magic. you are a well of love. be unashamed of your presence. be the entire book of your excellence, even if it is difficult and muddy. especially when it is difficult and muddy. you are en route, friend. take courage. the road is patient. the sky is open. feel everything and do not apologize for any of it.

yours,
tonya

Cincinnati, Ohio

the lady at church tells my mother
to keep it. i am the right kind
of bastard to be born
with an expiration. they collect the offering,
my mother fixing the nappy
into something decent before
she runs off to another stain. his name
have no meaning but the upkeep
in her swing tell me different. tell me
sunday got me here. and this
new man with brown lips is going
to make us stay. i have never been
to the bronx, never known what
kind of man could make
my mother leave
her god.

I Am Twenty-Two

i am 22 rocking the latest 85
always down for a diner
thrift shop educator
8 mile enthusiast
cincinnati bengals fan
if and when it will ever matter
kendrick lamar's hand is matrimony
the epitome of #thatawkwardmomentwhen
angela bassett's bestie
hater of all things hollister
a gryffindor or ravenclaw, but never the hufflepuff
the embodiment of olivia pope as patronus

i am in love with a boy
and his hand stitched guitar
i am in love with a boy
and his odd stitched heart
harmonizing in the key of lonely
i am mother's water broke in church pew
father's lost letter
daughter he will never meet
i am scared to be black
i am proud to be black
i have never seen the notebook
but have rewatched every installment of friday

i am metaphors that boost my street cred
because all i want in life
is to rap under the alias tonyasaurus-rex
i am bullet in an open flood

swimming in the junkyard
of the most sacred drowning
i am a girl still learning God

lupus is an autoimmune disease
this means that immune cells in the body
that usually attacks or destroys viruses
attacks healthy parts of the body:
skin, blood cells, kidneys, heart and brain
the cause is not known

common symptoms include
butterfly shaped rash across the bridge of the nose
sunlight sensitivity
arthritis
fatigue or depression

there is no cure for lupus
but most people can lead normal, active lives
with proper care

i am diagnosed
but have rewatched every installment of friday
because all i want in life
is to rap under the alias lupus
is an autoimmune daughter he will never meet
a thrift shop virus
this means that immune cells
in the body are scared
to be black

common symptoms include
harmonizing in the key of lonely
and the embodiment of olivia pope as patronus
i am a fan who is a cincinnati bengals disease
if and when it will ever matter

other parts of the body such as
skin, blood cells, kidneys , heart and brain
are always down for a diner
the cause of sensitivity is not known
i am in love with sunlight lupus
swimming in the junkyard of fatigue
that usually hollister all things hate and attack
i am a gryffindor, who began attacking the normal
parts of my body for never seeing the notebook
the butterfly shaped rash across the bridge
of depression
i am proud to be mother's water
broke in church pew
the epitome of #thereisnocure

i am 25 rocking the latest lupus
common symptoms are
metaphors that boost my odd stitched kidneys
stunning blood cells
wrecking brilliance of a brain
steel heart
good skin

most people can lead normal,
active lives without cure
with proper care
in an open flood
where the most sacred drowning
is the girl who is still learning God

While Sitting In Central Park I Consider My Mother's Good Knife

You and me and the devil makes three. Don't need no other lovin' babe. - Emmylou Harris

in my youth, i sat in parks
& watched

the runners,
a chorus of feet

the lone appearing
to be less alone

like myself,
right now

i try to become mine
but my demons—

thirst under the sun

&

no one wants you
no one wants you
no one wants you

Una Mujer y Su Casa / A Woman and Her House

there is a woman and there is her house. her house is its own map. the map is a saving of sacred things. a sacred thing is not letting go. letting go is another way of dying.

her house is a burial ground. people say words like "crazy." people say words without knowing their meaning. people say a lot, but do very little. the woman and her house are silent and loud. a charged echo. the house is a garden of loose objects. the woman is a keeper of the disposable.

once, the people helped the woman remove her sacred things from the house. once, the woman undid the work of the people. once, she stood alone, looking out of a window that reveals the holiness of living in imperfection.

there is a man who says, "there is no hope for the woman." there is a man whose frown rests like a coat hanger. i am sure the woman can see this from her house. i am sure she can see it all.

On A Too-Hot Wednesday

on a too-hot wednesday, i become naked
unravel the silk
remove the underwear
and lay in the drench of myself

i ask God to look away

i curl my finger into a country
and raid everything about me that is a home

first, there is uncertainty
the shame of a praying woman
then, there is a body
moving into itself, a body becoming
a hall of damp breath

what monuments can fit inside?
if there is a mountain before you,
will you climax?

will you clean your hands over and over?
remove the molasses. the sticky of unholy release

like God wasn't watching the whole time

A Scripture
For Delilah

i guess it is an awful pleasure
to masturbate to sadness.

holding a black umbrella
under the sun.

unhealthy, tiring
the hand.

wasteful labor,
little gain.

Thirteen, or, How OKCupid Told My Mother I Had the Devil Living Inside of Me

the first said, you must be a man
as much as you want this, then offered
a glass of water - as if to say,
have i not baptized you enough?

the second will know nothing
of your face but how low
your head can bow, how wide
your mouth can crucify.

the third is lazarus.
speaks only of what he can see.
there is God in that.

the fourth, an accent, eyes
as green as eden.

the fifth, blonde-haired whiskey,
hands like goliath, will toss you
because he does not believe
in your Christ, but you are still
pretty for a black girl.

the sixth, a dancer, will know
he is the age of Jesus at the cross,
will still make a resurrection
out of you.

the seventh will kiss you
only after he's allowed
his righteous work to rest
on your face, your chest.

the eighth is the driest valley
of lonely your bones ever laid in.

the ninth, a lower east side bar shot,
the reason you do not call home,
what has no welcome mat.

the tenth will ask if you are clean.

the eleventh will try to unlearn your scripture
leg by leg, lip by lip.

the twelfth is a rooftop in brooklyn
a bypassing thunderstorm in brooklyn
a hand job in brooklyn

thirteen: the number of men
you've allowed to wound your human
with their horns.
fornication disguised as forgiveness.
you swallowed thirteen men in two months
when you mistook night for lonely, but it is all
blasphemy. it is all reason to forget your mother

gave birth to you under sun and sin

so your throat is but a canal, but an ark.
your skin, a lustful fist.
you are the daughter of delilah.
always have been.

thirteen: one more disciple you've allowed
to holy bible spread you. not one of them black.

they will want to read you and convince their bod-
ies they walk on water. but it is all blasphemy.

it is one more who ransacked your gospel
before reading it, made you another

this is the first time
i've slept with a black girl
miracle.

Black Paralysis

in a dream, i lose all my teeth.
the boys i know wait for the slow spill of blood.

i bleach my dress in it
and say look. i strangle the softest
beasts, their manes caught in my throat.

not as an excuse for the thickness of the walls
when lonely tucks in its shirt and leaves

willingly,
i have fucked the worst of them.

you know, the kind you can see coming,
coming, coming

when you ask them not to.

The Most Poppin' Crotchet Braids

rose takes me out tonight because depression got a
big brag. i wear a just-right tight of a dress. grey.
magical in its ability to provide an ass where
there once was none. ain't that like God? to give
you what you been asking for in abundance?

i get into her car and we dish about the men we
keep within our grip. they emerge as the aint shit
inhabitants of the land of who da fuck do you think i
is and we laugh. it is roaring and daring. like good
sex for a table of two at red lobster.

rose is wearing a leopard print fur jacket and eve-
rything in downtown los angeles is a rapture. the
men with their crazed stares. the city exactly
where we want it.

we go into a bar and the bouncer ignores me for
what i assume is my negligence to return his text
and ain't that like a man? to give you what you
don't be asking for in abundance?

we order our drinks, our spirits. we move through
the crowd like Jesus, like gossip until we don't.
one man, young and lips wrought of gin, grabs my
hand like Jesus.

rose and i continue to the dance floor. i am stiff
even in the dark, but my two-step is on point.
thank God for the paper hand fan rose used for
the sweat a herd of grinding bodies can create.

a boy resembling evan peters approaches me and part of myself unfurls. he apologizes for his gluttony and again, like Jesus, i pardon him.

out of the women's bathroom comes a stunning hawk of a girl. she puts her hands into my hair, the most poppin' crotchet braids, and confesses her love for them, her worship of them. i am stiff.

rose removes the hand of the stunning hawk and the boy resembling evan peters continues to apologize. i look for the other black women in the bar. the others who have had their most poppin' hair become a raid. the bounce of their kink its own clapback.

and there are none, so i am not like Jesus this time. instead, i look back at the dj, sip on the glutton and ask, is this 2 chainz playing right now?

despite the
condition
of the soil,

i will choose to bloom.

The Blonde, The Boul- der & The Blues

white girl   acute & slick-like,

greased palm,

*no love,   you don't got that pull here   you don't
got your name until i spit it back at you. see
        how i beam? it's all spell, baby.*

it's all

        too easy. check the scoreboard.

hear those horns? that sax on the 3/5th of your human?

Drowning
(The Good Kind)

the balcony is love me
wingspan of brick
brooklyn church, stained glass
whisper

you deserve to drown

glory be
the dirt covered mouth
on the m train

last night he
was not worth it

to drown, again

in the handprint of a silly girl

her inability to stay above
the water.

The Black Girl Miracle & The 72 Hour Hold

consider your sadness
its familiar landscape—
the forests of gutted girls, like yourself
consider the boy who loves you back
and calls you a bitch
forced in the same octave
consider the hospital, its thick-walled religion
consider the cunt you are—
the kind worn by their father's backhand
the kind to give ugly its own sermon

you love that shit, right?
that believable sickness
that singed pulse
god damn, girl
look at your heart
why it thump so crooked?
why you blue so easy?

The Saddest Thing

is not the diagnosis.

how my body swell
like a loaded cannon.

not the iv sunk
into blood, a ready ship.

not the girl who could not
name the days of the week.

whose mind was camp
for anything blur.

it is not how i called death
a magnificent friend.

told him to take me
where he finds rest,

that i may know air
beyond a hospital.

the silence of another
thing wrong with me.

no. the saddest thing
is the body void of love.

for then, and only then,
do you go missing.

The Black Girl Miracle Swipes Right on Tinder

i .

in the car, we are a crass gleam of sweat. a hotbox
of mercy. he takes me as a fang into the nape. the
moon, a careful witness makes excuse for the in-
dulgence. "your black is forbidden," he says. it is
vacant, this clutch. it is full, this thirst. "sex is for
the dead," he says, and then, "what is your name?"

ii .

in the backseat of his blue rental car, the lust ran
like cyclone.   his red mouth, a lock. his
white, a cavity of smut. in the bank of flaw, they
are kin. my sick, a crave of meat. my lord, not far,
is too a puncture of grace. singing, "eat of this last
bargain. it will heal you. it will."

The Weekend

iii .

do not settle for temporary. for gust and bravado.
white teeth and iron gaze. white teeth, whiskey
stained. a fleeting stench. it is beg and howl. let
me in. never stay. i have heard this ballad once.
how they urge the communion. sip the wine.
break the bread. until ghost. they spite the way
you love. you too mercy for their head. you too
still for their reckon. call it bottomless caution.
incomplete. secondhand grace. but you are not
brief. you are endless brushfire. you are waking
brick. unheeding quake. you deserve the unrelent-
ing. you deserve the keep.

Proverbs Four: Train

lord, here lies a grudge.
i beg the earth to show me its venom.
i unlearn its bite.
what it is to erase a man and his transit.
what it is to avoid burnside avenue.

lord, my lone hands cannot know sex
without the risk of nicotine.

lord, my man cannot know my sex
without the risk of trauma.

come home, darling.
there is a remedy in the fold
of your grandmother's laugh.

stay there.

I Know the Cold Touch of the Living

i know the cold touch of the living.
i know to ignore its brass, haunting
jaw. the prying mouth of air
wants to take away my wild, but i want
to be in love with he who will not
make a roast of my body. i want to
hold the man made of rain. his name
is son of knife. his hands, most
gentle wind chime. excuse me,
for i have made a mockery
of lust. i have named the story, Girl
of a Thousand Apologies.
it reads as a cautionary tale. it reads, i am
The Bastard of Summer.
a stunning poison.
how they drink of me.
but i say, blessed is the river's bite.
it will keep me until the depression
quiets like the tempest. my God
as my witness, i fuck up
when the wind is sharp. mother,
tell me there is pretty in burning
so divine, it is no longer guilt.

When The Lights Go Down

First of all, you talk white. Second off, you talk like you haven't give up yet. - Childish Gambino

If you woke up this morning feeling _____, know that it is okay to take time for yourself. If you woke up being called out of your name, reclaim who you are. If you find yourself not wanting to leave your bed, make a cup of hot tea and watch your favorite television show. If you feel alone, that is okay too. But before the day is done, call someone for two minutes or for two hours. We can't get through this without you. You, whose heart is constantly sinking. You don't have to 'get it together' right now. It is okay to be the ugliest cry in the room. To sit and be confused. I write this to you, dear friends, because today is abnormal. It is coffee thrown against the wall. An poised mourning. Just know, wherever you are and whenever you read this, I thought of you and said to myself, "me too, friend. me too."

The Black Girl Miracle Deletes Her Tinder Profile

i have kissed men made of drink and flirt,
wrote them poems.

let me show you my hands.
honest from the biting and the heartache.
honest from childhood's holy brawl .

once, i let it tell me the story
of how my grandparents met
and where love goes
when it is exhausted.

once, i begged for thunder
to keep the lonely from knocking,
to keep ugly from governing this town.

i know how to hold the night, rid my clothes,
to dance like everything about me is a marvel.

i know my insecurity:
the stretch marks,
the worn knuckles,
the pull of my skin,
the map it forms around my hips,
where it leads

come with me.
i know where we can make home
of this sin.

my name is flood.
and it is okay to be the wreck
if that is how we get to shore.

Here Is What Loneliness Tells You

you are the only one. you are the girl who feels awkward referring to herself as a woman. because some part of you is unable to grow into it. unable to launch melancholy to the west and leave it in an ocean. you are the good girl. always the good girl and the quiet kick. you are the girl who finds men who need only to loan your body for the night. you are one night. never morning. you are house party and shadow and hard hands that know how to travel. you are a girl who travels, alone. for poems. for crying. for high. aren't you tired of writing about faceless men? all who want your words. all of them made of grin, cheek and game. all of them some kind of actor. of slow exhaustion. slow fading. you are the girl who texts too much. you are made of too much. and so, you deserve ignore. an uber home. you deserve 'but we had a good time.' because what more are you made of? what more than the good. its anchor. its slingshot. its online dating app. its aimless run. you are the girl who runs. into the same ocean. where you left grief before you grew into it.

Here Is What Love Tells You

you are yours before you choose anyone else. you are cicada and buzz. loose flannel and cupped green tea. you are soft knuckles. the kind to know warmth. like dawn. you are dance alone. you are unafraid of alone. it is acoustic. the rain. it is his name and its irrelevance. it is your name and its blossom. its awaken. it is run to the ocean. and there is no sadness. and there is no sadness. and there is no sadness. you are growing. a woman. a woman who knows her name.

One Time For The Kid In The Back Of The Classroom Who Stayed Up Playing NBA2K17 Instead Of Doing Homework

After Jeremy Radin's, This Heaven Of Mud

Lord, bless this finite magic
bless the storyline
bless the good mundane
the bulk of the day
spent on rearranging furniture
in the sims: deluxe edition

bless the xbox, the playstation, the uploaded ver-
sion of snake on my nokia 3310 and its somewhat
metaphor on what it means for returning to one-
self

bless our thumbs, Lord, oh holy workers
of the gaming faith, worn by adventure
and the animation of truth
bless our villains and their phantom disbelief:
bowser, the mine in minecraft, and that one shape
in tetris that won't take a hint

bless the call of duty, black ops stealth,
the halo: spartan strike stillness

Lord, bless the mortal kombat victor, the fatality
bless the finish him,
how it soars through the body
like an unswept miracle

bless my brothers, conductors of this fancy
how they weld the unreal into flight
grand theft auto masterchefs,
professors of the cheat code
Lord, bless the cheat codes, the necessary temptation
tion

bless pacman and the ghosts we banquet
bless zelda and lara croft and princess peach
because intersectional feminism is about that life

bless the holiday of recreation,
bless the control, Lord, the God at our fingers
bless the characters
how we peel into avatar
our remains left at joystick's hinge

bless the levels and their unlocked boom, Lord
may they shout me into completed missions
may i gain the skill of power

bless the health points,
the second chance,
the grace in finally getting it right
bless it, Lord, the grace

your toolshed of compassion
as i run from an apostles of zombies
knocking at my good brain

bless the crooked assassin,
the barrel slinging gorilla, the e.
honda, the cincinnati bengals

bless our goliaths, Lord

send me with a couple of rocks and a healthy aim
these hands, fine blacksmiths of the button press

bless the video game
the familiar escape
the glorious distraction
the spontaneous bringing

bless me in this room of nintendo enthusiasts,
arcade specialists of a little less lonely

Lord, bless my lonely and the people i hide from
i am ready for less loneliness, Lord

jubilee will sprout from an unwashed couch
until i am the high scorer,
a minimized celebration, respectful
of my roommate's noise complaints
against my elegant wail
at the tv set

RuPaul Gives The Black Girl Miracle Her First Lesson In Realness

how can i be a black woman in this fierce world
and not have needs? i know what it is to be
the crash and current of the sea, honey. to shelter
my own villain and pronounce its hope. but
i say, take my love as the good mundane.
as the extraordinary silence, the fahrenheit.
to be in love with another is to be an open door.
to be in love with yourself is to be the whole damn
house.

Beyoncè Gives The Black Girl Miracle Her First Lesson In Healing

and in this moment i remember being teased for what is celebrated. and in this moment i beckon the girl i was and lift her as a call to resurrection. i give her this track and tell her to shake loose, oh sweet one. unravel yourself. be the hype they will never give you. they don't know your sorcery. they don't know the blues. they don't know a tired head from long nights of wanting to delete the black. they can't clutch what is a presence, snatching haters in its wake. you awake, oh sweet one. you been woke. been the slay. been the drop low. been mother's side eye. been summertime double dutch. been loving like you don't have time for a sorry. and there is something about this unshakeable grit, in this moment, with these braids and this melanated glow and these bottles of tabasco and my folk. witness the parade. sit on the front porch. the space is plenty. the lemons are ripe.

Hot Sauce In Our Bag

we are the slay   we are country   we are

hot comb and curling iron   we

are stretch mark   we are eco and mother

   we are runway and supreme court

justice   we are academy award and nobel

peace prize   we are malala

yousafzai   we are sophia dejesus   we are

 mascara   we are bitten nail

we are angelou promise   we keep our last

name   we courageous   we

are not asking for it   we bald   we locks

   we louboutin and timberland

we are reproductive rights   we college degree

and uppercut fist   we are

survivors   breast cancer   sexual assault

   domestic violence

we survive everyday   we are sari   we are

kente   we harlem gossip we are

quinceanera   we are widow and basket

weavers   we are

nina simone blackbird   we khaleesi   we

native   we are siren and bruja

we choose who we love   we fight for our love

   our names carrying the land and its wonder

I Am Twenty-Five

i am borrowed glory
and late-night diner runs
the city where i had my first kiss

i am a lesson in swimming
i am all of my dead
and the eulogies we hum

i am a mess of stillness
i am holding on
caught in the gust
of my curiosity
the strangers i mistake
for lovers and the dirt
underneath my nails

i am sorry
still trying to figure it out
the wild thing that i am
a hymnal bashed out
on a broken organ

For Him | Prologue or How My Grandparents Explain 46 Years Of Marriage

Grandpa: I was a slim and trim guy, then I married your grandma. Now look at me. She fed me good.

Grandma: (Laughing): Oh, James.

For Him | Act I

whisper to your lover how once
the body was not made of magic, but of rot.
prepare a lament, a soft cry
for the girl you were on occasion.
the black girl you apologize for once being.
the kind who cleansed
with white men, mirroring
her mother, a particular crime of nature.

remind yourself of slow attempts at bourbon.
tell him where you store the remains.
bring him the mold, the stories,
the count of those before him.
how they made you something biblical.
something of lazarus.
something out of the half-bit mouth of lonely.

explain to your lover your thoughts, all of them.
the one made of regret.
and he will make The Past
and will ask of the ways you love him.
you will weep as a house weeps
for every room you've been in
and did not wish to stay.
for your womb, your faulty womb
and the children you may not be able to make.

lover, how you knew this
and still speak their names.
there is no script for how i love you.

for the bronx, how it built our gravity, our ground.
for your mind, a wilderness of Badu and Big Pun.
for your heart, how it makes me better.
how depression becomes a swamp.

speak to me as the wind and i will hear you.
i will run my fingers kindly through your hair.
i will run kindly as the stream.

love the sin out of me.
love the sun into me.
hold me as the high waters.
for i have known my body to be a sewage
but with you i am learning it to be a well.

to be in love
during a
time of
injustice

is a
revolutionary
act.

Joy In The Year of Kidney Failure

is the sound of july in the bronx,
where fire hydrants become
waterfalls. the youngins, the black
and brown of them, bellowing
like newly shined trumpets in the sun.

is the night dust of accra
and the sweet mouth of a boy
with skin like tangerine.

is the initial devour into your favorite
burger and the juices runneth over
like the burger gods heard
your hungry cry for an endless
helping of pickles.

it is the destiny's child hit single
bills, bills, bills and it is 1999
and you are eight and completely
clueless as to what a bill actually is.

it is a gushing field of dandelions
and you are a spring dress
asking to be taken with the howl.

it is taking off your bra
after a long day's work.

is each time lupita nyong'o
takes a photograph.

and when the diagnosis is no longer
the smoke signal, but the calm
in what it means to be good to you.

An Open Letter To My Depression

I think the saddest people always try their hardest to
make people happy because they know what it's like to
feel absolutely worthless and they don't want anyone
else to feel like that. - Robin Williams

yesterday, i cried enough to name myself the sad
girl again. waiting for any boy again. who is igno-
rant to the splendid pace of my run. how my love
is sometimes a coward. and, after that, thirteen
men becomes another number. and after that
lonely develops a sex and an authority and after
that, my thoughts are family. always fussin' about
the wrong i have done. about the pretty i burned.
what i learned of sadness is from you.

you childhood friend
you midnight backtalk
got all the answers, right?
hold my wrists and this blade, right?
you want these veins, this blood
a red river i cannot swim in
you met me, twelve years old, weeping
you met me, twelve year old, molested
you unseen leech
unknown father
find nearest ledge
say walk out
say suspend
say wouldn't i be happier dead?
you slick tongue

animal of gossip
golden gate bridge
train station platform
my mother's good knife

loving you got me sick
got me suicide watch
got me blue pill
you tell me boy won't love me
but a fastened rope can
you tell me lupus is incurable
can't have seven children
can't be hospitalized three times
in one year and call that healing
you're a contradiction
a house of lies

sickness can do that, ya know
it can lie
it can claw
reverse the body until it is fickle
until my fear grows fangs
it will rattle in the dark and
truth be told
my sadness is a sour bullet
a spiraling bloom
it will not cease
it will not quiet
and i am afraid to die
        i am afraid to die

depression is a house of teeth
it will write you into a story without rest
it will kin you
comb your mouth into a haunting
name it a vacant wilderness

but dare yourself, extraordinary human
to run into unbolted joy screaming
    you cannot have me
    you cannot have me
    i am not my past
    i am not yesterday's shame
    i am worthy of love
    i am worthy

i forgive the people
who are not strong enough to believe in me
kicking into the sky like it is the only way up

Until The Stars Collapse

you owe it to yourself to quit being the apology. to hold your hand and sing your favorite song. to love another and see how far that will go. to love yourself and forget where you were headed in the first place. love is a funny story. it wakes up and builds a plot. it wakes up and shapes you into the kind of woman your mother studies. i am not perfect in it. i am not even remotely articulate. but it is big, this love. it is airborne and triumphant. i am no easy show. i hurt like the climb of my lineage. i hurt on purpose. i hurt to not be hurt. no, none of this is an excuse. just a blueprint. a map. come find me when the day is bronze and the sorrow is full. i am building my poem in this here heart. all of it is a working title.

The Black Girl Miracle & The 72 Hour Hold (Continued)

they will put her in the straitjacket and ask how
she tightened the buckle. she did not have a de-
mon. she is tired of stigma. she is tired of being on
the back burner. she is tired of being useful and
used. of having to be her own survival. her own
healing circle. when she decides to speak up, to
deny unwanted advances, to fight for her children,
to fight for herself, to wear and be and navigate
this life as she desires, it is often met with a
dangerous rhetoric. one drenched in death. she
is truly other worldly. what shape her body
must endure to be both at the frontline of
fighting for justice and at the bottom of ever re-
ceiving it. what it will mean when they say she
brought this upon herself. when they revisit the
psychiatric hospital and say she had it coming.
how despite this, she must choose to be an unde-
niable force of a black woman. a storm everyone
was prepared for and yet chose to ignore its fore-
cast.

For Him | Act II

i am not holy yet   my hands have filth in their
creases   enough to make sickness into a proverb
i have been hiding in the trunk of my mother's old
love   i am sometimes a fool for how big i let
my heart get—bastard case
give me your name   and i will return a for-
giveness   that will ask,

what were we even arguing about?

do not
abbreviate
who you are.
be the
expanded
version of your
marvel.

be the
story they
cannot put
down.

For Her | Finale

it's not that i fell in love and found the cure.
no, it's that i met love and began to heal.

curtain call.

The Black Girl Miracle Saw Moonlight & Cannot Stop Crying

Thought of the baptism at age thirteen. Thought of the blue my black becomes when cast at dusk. Want to be an ocean holding the scared black girl I was and sometimes still am. Want to cast the mouth of the body that does not know my body and wants to hurt it. Take me home, glorious sea. Take my love, treasured rain. Wash the guilt. Overwhelm my stains. I am becoming. I am the untold. I am a family of weeping and that too is a baptism. This morning, I will wash my face in warm waters and pretend to be something more than drowning.

On Being Called A Slave During My Acting Class

the invisible cackle
sits in the slaughter
a family of loose guns
a reason to swim when
all else is a sunken place

it is blurred line,
everything can't be good, girl
everything can't be this much animal
and not get bit,

i am always at the mercy
of white teeth

a born anthem
to be made in this skin

the cure is to keep
shading so black
you'd have no choice
but to watch and say,

goddam, what did i miss?

Dear Discouraged

With all that is real and difficult in this life. With
the news, the death, the sighs that fill our conver-
sations, I want to urge the value in taking care of
ourselves. In taking care of each other. So please,
post that selfie if it means we can find something
beautiful in the ruin. Go out for a drink with the
homies. Be a grand libation. Download Pokemon
Go and meet someone new. Allow yourself to be
angry. Go to McDonalds and yes, devour those
fries without shame. Dab until your arm is ex-
hausted. Sit by the ocean. If you're anything like
me, learn how to ride a bike. Weep in the bath-
room. Weep on the train. Weep in the arms of
someone who gets it. Go to a store and try on
something that you cannot afford right now, but
treat yourself to the idea of embracing what seems
impossible. Be in love. Be in love. Be in love. Be in
love. Be in love. Be in love. With yourself, always
first. Support your friends. Read a romance novel.
Write 16 bars. Watch a non-sensical amount of cat
videos. Buy a stranger a meal. You've got hugs,
give them out for free. Stay in bed. Dammit, dance
like everyone is watching. Dance like everything is
lit. Holy dust, you are here.

The world may be slipping from your grasp, but you've
got a storm of goodness behind you. I would be lying if I
said it is easy. If I said our trauma isn't something that
needs to be checked on often. If I said finding joy
isn't a full-time occupation. Yes, I hear you. This
is not a means of ignoring what is reality. No, this
is living despite it all. This is a gospel of sorts.
You, something more than miracle. Us, turning
water into rebirth.

The Black Girl Miracle Tells Her Sister A Secret On The Corner Of 183rd Street & Walton Avenue

Come celebrate with me that everyday something has tried to kill me and has failed. - Lucile Clifton

Today I wrestle with my boyfriend while Donald Trump is sworn into presidency. A bad joke. My kitten joins us on the bed and bare light peeks through our window. It is cold in the Bronx. Everything is a numb hand learning how to practice feeling.

I watch as the country folds into the arch of his brow. There is a red sea of red hats. And the word God whistles like a river in Mississippi. Like a freedom no longer a freedom.

I imagine that even the rain would like to protest. Like somehow our ghosts have come to weep. Like our future has come to warn us.

The bible speaks of revelation and the earth swallowed whole to its end. The bible speaks at his inauguration of a kingdom come. Of a will done. And their hands clap. And the choir is the pulse of America. And the teapot I put on the stove is boiling like the land.

There is fear. Where my body reveals its name in a different language to distract its origin. How every white man I've taken into this body has had a mouth similar in his shape. Has had an opinion similar in his politics.

There is anger. I hold my love and ask for its purge. To cleanse me. Once. To cleanse me. Again. Until I am a miracle and not the salt I can become if I look back. I pour my country into our mother's house and that is a national anthem. That is an opulent resistance.

Do not sour your heart by the ugly they make into sermon. Into law. Into history. Do not unlearn the royalty of your unhinged light. You are a threat, they will say. But they would have confused you for an eclipse. For how much black space you will behold.

And the hopelessness will come. But do not surrender. And they will want to touch your hair. But do not allow them. And they will want and always want, but you are the genesis. Amen.

You are the daughter of raised fists. Amen.

You are the work learning how to be done. Amen.

You are afraid and brilliant and necessary. Amen.

Love yourself.
Love yourself.
Love yourself.

You are running,
a black girl, into
her own.   Amen.

Thank You:

Mom, my favorite recipe. I will win the world for you.
Grandma, you are the phone call I look forward to, the
kind of grace found in the gospel. Let's two-step to
Smokey Robinson this summer. Vanessa, this entire book
is for you. Find it when you need it most. May your hon-
esty keep me honest. Charles, I will put money on your
gamer skills any day. I have got that faith in you, brother.
Always have and always will. Tony, the tallest laugh in the
room. Remember black beans? Keep leading, baby broth-
er. Keep finding the comedy in the heaviness. Grandpa,
my favorite storyteller. You remind me to speak up, to be
known. You allow me to be visible. Uncle Jerry, thank you
for Mickey Mouse.

Marchelle, my Los Angeles mom. I do not know where to
begin. I survived because of you. I survive because of you.
May you dance across the world. May you never stop bath-
ing in sound, in love. Sarita, it was meant to be. Bachelor
nation marathons, grocery shopping tips, glorious kinship.
Aziza, thank you for the second home. Thank you Barnes
family for your unending kindness, for chai tea, for Dory.

Alyesha, sisterhood is real because you have shown it to
me. Galactic poetry slam, soon? King, my Beyoncé com-
rade, my side-eye best-friend, my little big sister. Healing
will know your name. Laryssa, where do I even start? Gha-
na, NYU, late-night braiding sessions, church visits. You
are stuck with me forever. Janelle, when you win your first
Oscar, I will be twerking in my living room. Your friend-
ship is Dole's pineapple ice cream. It is everything to me.

Rose, Los Angeles was a little less lonely because of you. Shihan, my spades partner, my coach, my friend. I am still working on that play. Manny, ramen burgers to audition advice, you are one of a kind. Suzanne, you are the type of fierce I aspire to. You challenge me. You hold me. You believe in me.

Simone, people like you don't come around often. Thank you is not enough. Michelle, we saw Beyoncé live and you tolerate my farts. Mama Bears for life. Lili, you taught me survival, how to fight, how to live. Maria, from high-school to post-grad, you tolerate my humor [insert umm yeah here]. Thank you for growing with me. Amy, I learn from you the dance of forgiveness and the meaning of self-love. Sean, you are my brother. I will always keep you close. Venessa, my khalessi, my teammate for life.

Mahogany, many slams and memories later, I am grateful for the times you saved me from myself, for Paris, for the poems that made me better.

Kanwal, you remind me to laugh, to reach and to know the amazing taste of digestives. Big hugs to you and your precious family.

Sidney, thank God we both swiped right.

Through the chemotherapy, the donations, the moments of self-doubt, the reasons to celebrate, the hospitalizations, the laughter over dinner, the loneliness, the necessary conversations, thank you for your friendship:

Anaïs Aïda, Rotana Tarabzouni, JP Saxe, Jamie Tworkowski and the entire To Write Love On Her Arms team, Claire Biggs, Jessica Tworkowski Haley, Michael Cirelli, Urban Word NYC, Da Poetry Lounge, Get Lit, Nuyorican Poetry Café, New York University, Valerie Cabral, Crystal Valentine, Gabriel Ramirez, Amari Tims, Sierra DeMulder, Matthew Cuban Hernandez, Giddy Perez, Jon Foreman, Keith Tutt, Natyna Bean, Buddy Wakefield, Beau Sia, Cynthia Lester, Danielle Bennett, Harmony Holiday, Denise Boneta, Shirley Zhang, Amrit Singh, Susie Chan, Haley Houseman, Jasmine Mans, Kyland Turner, Bryan Dale, Jasmine Williams, Angelo Tommie, Dominique Christina, Yazmin Watkins, Patrisse Khan-Cullors, Dominique Toney, Daniella Watson, Malcolm Wicks, Dawn Salmon, Otis College of Art and Design, Shefali Mistry, Mario Mesquita, Noé Gaytán, Carol Zou, Estephany Campos Garcia, Claudia Borgna, Catherine Scott, Beth Ann Morrison, Jeanette Degollado, Dana Duff, Chelo Montoya, Karen Moss, Henderson Blumer, Jaha Zainabu, Mariette Hartley, Project UROK, The American Foundation for Suicide Prevention, The Lupus Foundation of America, New York Cares, Gary Bagley, Beth Lehmann, Keren Segal, Laura Tucker, Cynthia Wong, Elizabeth Leheny, Erin Wietecha, Caroline Rothstein, Fisseha Moges,

Health Opportunities High School, Dr. Clark, Diamond Wynn, Malanya Graham, Carvens Lissaint, Aaron Samuels, Jess X. Snow, Yarminiah Rosa, Shamika Mcburney, Jordan Wilson, Jessica & David Ospino, Greg & Libni Francis, Patricia Wilkins, B.A.S.I.C.S International, Christ Tabernacle & the block that raised me— 183rd Street and Walton Avenue.

To the people who follow my work, who continue to shares their stories and find home in the meaning of my words, I cherish you to the moon and beyond. Wherever you are, may the sun hold you close and may love know your name.

Lastly, thank you not a cult press for this magical ride. Thank you Daniel Lisi for the invitation. Thank you Jeremy Radin and Safia Elhillo for your continued patience and brilliance.

I am made possible by the mercy and grace of God, forever learning the love that gave me life.

About the Author

Tonya Ingram is the 2011 New York Knicks Poetry Slam champion, a member and co-founder of NYU's poetry slam team, a member of the 2011 Urban Word-NYC team, the 2013 Nuyorican Grand Slam team and the 2015 Da Poetry Lounge Slam team. She is a six-time poetry slam finalist, a 2014 Pushcart Prize nominee and the author of Growl and Snare. Her work has traveled throughout the United States, Ghana, The Literary Bohemian, Huffington Post, Amy Poehler's Smart Girls, LupusChick.com, For Harriet, Buzzfeed, Afropunk, Rude Magazine, Cultural Weekly, Marie Claire Italia, The WILD, Upworthy, To Write Love On Her Arms, Youtube and season four of Lexus Verses and Flow. Her work focuses on the intersectionality of art as healing and art as awareness about mental and physical health. She has shared the stage with Hill Harper, Soledad O' Brien, President Clinton, Anthony Hamilton, Lynn Whitfield, and others. She is a New York University alumna, a Cincinnati native, a Bronx-bred introvert and is a recent graduate from Otis College of Art & Design where she obtained her MFA in Public Practice. Her first full length book of poetry, Another Black Girl Miracle, is now available through not a cult press.

CPSIA information can be obtained
at www.ICGtesting.com
Printed in the USA
FSOW02n0613120617
34987FS